101 GREAT IDEAS

TO CREATE A CARING GROUP

A SMALL GROUP RESOURCE BY

THOM CORRIGAN

NAVPRESS®

BRINGING TRUTH TO LIFE

OUR GUARANTEE TO YOU

We believe so strongly in the message of our books that we are making this quality guarantee to you. If for any reason you are disappointed with the content of this book, return the title page to us with your name and address and we will refund to you the list price of the book. To help us serve you better, please briefly describe why you were disappointed. Mail your refund request to: NavPress, P.O. Box 35002, Colorado Springs, CO 80935.

The Navigators is an international Christian organization. Our mission is to reach, disciple, and equip people to know Christ and to make Him known through successive generations. We envision multitudes of diverse people in the United States and every other nation who have a passionate love for Christ, live a lifestyle of sharing Christ's love, and multiply spiritual laborers among those without Christ.

NavPress is the publishing ministry of The Navigators. NavPress publications help believers learn biblical truth and apply what they learn to their lives and ministries. Our mission is to stimulate spiritual formation among our readers.

ISBN 1-57683-072-1

Unless otherwise identified, all Scripture quotations in this publication are taken from the *HOLY BIBLE: NEW INTERNATIONAL VERSION* ® (NIV®). Copyright © 1973, 1978, 1984 by International Bible Society, used by permission of Zondervan Publishing House, all rights reserved. The other version used is *The Message* (MSG) by Eugene H. Peterson, copyright © 1993, 1994, 1995, 1996, used by permission of NavPress Publishing Group.

Printed in the United States of America

4 5 6 7 8 9 10 11 12 13 14 15 / 09 08 07 06 05

FOR A FREE CATALOG OF NAVPRESS BOOKS & BIBLE STUDIES, CALL 1-800-366-7788 (USA). IN CANADA, CALL 1-800-839-4769.

Contents

PART TWO: CARING IN YOUR GROUP

PART THREE: CARING OUTSIDE YOUR GROUP

PART FOUR: CARING AS A GROUP

I would like to dedicate this book to all those people who allowed me to learn to care for them in small groups over the years.

I also want to dedicate this work to my daughters—Molly, who is a lover of people, and Stephanie, who is learning to let God care for her in new ways—who help make up the small group in our home.

Introduction

I've been asked whether this is a collection of ideas to help small group leaders care for the members of their groups, or to teach group members how to care for each other. The answer is both. People learn best when what is discussed is also modeled. Leaders who care well for people are likely to produce groups full of caring people. If a leader uses one of the ideas in this book to care for his or her members, and at appropriate moments explains what's going on, chances are high that members will start doing the same things and even generating their own creative ideas for caring.

This resource grew out of many years of leading and participating in groups of all sizes, shapes, and varieties. Some of these Great Ideas were forged on the anvil of hard-knocks, after really messing up. Others came from watching skilled leaders at work, and trying to emulate what I saw them do in my setting. Some of them came from the very people I was (or currently am) trying to lead and serve.

I've learned a lot from the dozens of groups I have led over the past twenty-two years, but the biggest thing I have learned is this: God loves the church and desires to care for His sons and daughters. Being invited into partnership with Him and having the opportunity to care for some of his people is one of the greatest blessings we can receive. Jesus left us this simple command that sums up who we are to be to one another, "A new command I give you: love one another. As I have loved you, so you must love one another. All men will know that you are my disciples if you love one another" (John 13:34-35).

A few years ago a good friend of mine, Pastor Ed McGuigan, told me a story about a young couple preparing for their first child. Deciding to transform their extra bedroom into a nursery, they remodeled the entire room, replacing the carpet, wallpaper, and drapery. Then they carefully shopped for and purchased a new crib, changing table, decorative lamps, and several mobiles to hang around the room for their child's amusement. Finally, everything was ready for their new baby.

Before long the delivery date arrived and the newest addition to their family was placed with great care into her welcoming crib.

A few days later, as the new mother walked down the hallway toward the baby's room, she noticed her husband standing just inside the doorway, staring into the crib. She stood and watched him for a few moments, then walked up behind him, placed her arm around his waist and said, "Honey, a penny for your thoughts." Without turning to look at her, still gazing into the crib he responded excitedly, "Isn't it amazing—almost miraculous—how anyone can manufacture and sell a crib like this for only $89.95!?"

We need to remind ourselves from time to time that, while the mechanics and process of leading a group are really important, caring for the people and loving them in Jesus' name is our calling. With that in mind, here are 101 of the best "care-giving" ideas I've run across. I hope these ideas—and the many more I'm sure you will come up with—will give you joy as you serve God's people in a small group setting.

PART ONE:

Caring for Your Group

1
Help Them
Think Outside the Box

Regardless of our age, occupation, or experience, we are creatures of habit. If we're not careful, habit can lead to lives that lack creativity. Learning how to be creative is not hard—it is an attitude and a willingness to try new things and to think in new and different ways.

Challenge the members of your group to try a different way of doing activities and tasks that have become a regular part of your group process. Challenge them to begin by driving to or from the group on a different route, and to be aware of what is happening in the world around them! Then ask for a report. They may be amazed at what they notice.

Occasionally change the order of various parts of your group meeting. "We always do it this way" and "We never did it that way before" can indicate that you are in a rut. Try subtle changes in your process and delivery. Remind the group of the positive things that can happen when we put ourselves in the frame of mind to be aware of God in our midst, and expect Him to do a work among us.

2
Send a Note of Encouragement

It's always great to get home at the end of a long day and find a personal note from someone offering a word of encouragement.

It takes just a few moments to write a note, and you can cover the whole group in a few months by writing one a week. If you invite the group to get involved (as in Telephone Calls, Idea number 67), everyone will get a note in the same time period!

With the growing popularity of e-mail, it is even easier to send a note to someone. Without the usual restraints of regular mail—buying a card, finding a stamp, driving to the post office—sending an e-mail message is almost as easy as preparing a cup of tea. In my groups, we pass around an address list that includes the e-mail addresses of everyone who has one.

I find that just a simple greeting and a note to remind the person that I appreciate them, or a scripture reference, or letting them know I am praying for them, can really turn a person's day around or add the finishing touch to a day that is going well. Don't get caught up in the idea that you have to spend a lot of time (or money) to do this right. Just do it, and the people in your group are sure to appreciate it.

3
Help Them Learn to Deal With Difficult People

I have led many groups and have encountered some interesting individuals in those groups. Each time a person who was difficult to live with, who lacked certain social skills, or who expressed inappropriate behavior started attending the group, we were presented with a decision. We could decide to love, accept, and forgive this person, or we could let him know that he made us uncomfortable and eventually drive him away from our group. I am proud to say that most of the time our group took the high road and determined to accept the person regardless of where she had been, what she had done (or was doing) or how she presented herself.

I believe one function of the small group is to act like a triage unit and outpatient clinic. We cannot allow destructive and divisive behaviors (verbal attacks, sexual advances, et cetera), but we can handle many of the issues that people struggle with if we offer grace and mercy. As a leader, you need to have sufficient boundaries in place so that you do not take ownership of a person's problems, but you can surely project an attitude of support and encouragement, speaking the truth in love. It is often possible to protect the whole group's safety without ejecting someone who makes others uncomfortable.

God has entrusted to us a sacred responsibility to love and care for His people. It is a blessing to see a group invest in a member who has had a rough life, has been abused, or simply lacks skills to interact in pleasant and healthy ways. Our groups show their distinction over other groups of people by the way we compassionately reach out to the lost, the broken, the prodigal, and the outcast. We have an opportunity to offer a safe, redemptive place. You may need to refer some people to a pastor, counselor, or other caregiver for issues you are not capable of dealing with, but the group can definitely be a safe port in the storm for anyone who wants to get well and grow as a child of God.

4

Send Birthday Cards

For many people, birthdays are important events. Take the time to find out the birthday of each of the people in your group. Write down their birthdays on your calendar at home or in your day planner. Just a simple note or prayer for blessing in an inexpensive card can be a highlight in someone's day!

I have asked a volunteer in my group to take on the responsibility for accumulating some personal information from each person. This includes birthdays and anniversaries. You can ask this "scribe" to prepare a greeting card the week before the event and quietly ask all the other group members to sign the card. Boxes of cards can be purchased from assortment card companies without spending a lot of money, and a simple card can have a great impact.

5
Keep Confidences

Knowing you are a "safe" person who can be confided in, and who will keep a confidence, is a treasure. In this day of unidentified "leaks" at all levels, it is great to know your group leader (and fellow group members) will keep confidential anything and everything you share in the group. Because it is so essential, group confidentiality is worth talking about several times a year. It establishes and reinforces the safety net that people need in order to share their private thoughts, feelings, and experiences.

I encourage every group to develop a group covenant. This simple set of ground rules can be a life saver and help keep your group on track. Included in the covenant should be a statement about confidentiality. It can read something like this: "We will practice the covenant of confidentiality: Whatever is shared here, stays here." By designing and discussing the various aspects of your group covenant, you have the opportunity to fully deliberate the issues involved in keeping confidences.

As the leader, you should model confidentiality and be known as a safe person. I have known many a leader who violated confidence by "sharing a concern" with other leaders. I have seen great damage done by well-meaning people who shared prayer requests outside the group and effectively violated the trust others had placed in them.

We have a rule of thumb for confidentiality: The only time anything will be shared outside the group is if a member shares a plan to harm himself or another, or shares a story about abusing a child, an elderly person, or a mentally/physically challenged person. In those cases we are required morally and legally to report the danger or abuse to those in authority in our church or organization. Even then we are bound by confidentiality and will share only that which is pertinent to this issue. Confidence is a treasure that should be guarded.

6
Give Honest Evaluations

Evaluations can be broken into two categories. First, if you are supervising a person or apprenticing her in some capacity either in the group or outside, telling the truth in love will contribute significantly to the person's spiritual growth. Giving honest evaluations of progress is a way to reflect a reality that may otherwise be confusing or distorted in the person's mind.

Second, if someone lists you as a reference for a job or some other kind of contract, it is important to give an honest evaluation, without expanding on his capabilities or understating his lack. We live in a society where the truth is relative, so it is essential for us as Christian leaders to state the truth. I often will call the person to tell them what I have said or written on an evaluation for a prospective employer. They then have the opportunity to give me some feedback or choose whether to use me as a reference in the future.

7
Tell the Truth

One way to tell people the truth is to find good things and areas of growth in their lives to point out to them. Nobody gets more encouragement than he needs. Encouragement is different from making someone feel okay or trying to puff him up. Rather, it finds a way to bless through telling him the truth.

Another time to tell the truth is when people do something wrong—when they are mistaken or fall into sin. When you see someone failing in an area or misbehaving, simply take him aside (after you have prayed and considered your own life) and in simple terms, tell him the truth about what you are seeing. Remind him that you love and accept him, and that you are willing to help him through the process by praying for him, by pointing out scriptures, and by suggesting resources and books that he can purchase to help give him understanding. To tell the truth in love is to serve a person.

Honesty is increasingly rare. If you cannot be truthful, do not speak. It is better to be thought of as dull than to be known as less than truthful. Be truthful in the small things, and it will spill over to larger issues. Choose not to walk in "gray" areas. Light separates the darkness, and we are called to walk in the light. Be aware that your leadership is being scrutinized by those whom you lead. Your life as well as your words speak volumes about what is in your heart.

8
Be Loyal

Many people have never experienced loyalty from another person. In our culture, if you don't like something, you go shopping somewhere else to find it. That attitude flows over to the church. In a small group, we have an opportunity to extend loyalty—that is, to stay with people through the good and the bad times, and to stick with them when they are in crisis. Being loyal sets an example, and so teaches others to be loyal. It also gives them hope of a God who will stick with them no matter what they do, where they've been, or what they've done.

9
Offer Accountability

When offered and accepted, accountability can be a gift. Offering to hold people accountable to their goals, commitment to change, or growth in responsibility can help them stick to the purposes they feel called to.

Mutual accountability is usually easier to commit to. When accountability is one-sided or feels more like being monitored than encouraged, it is hard to follow through with. When a person knows that you, too, are being held accountable for your growth, mentoring and disciplemaking become more attainable.

10
Be Supportive

Sometimes all a person needs to succeed in a task or to overcome a barrier in her life is a little support. Take an interest in what she is going through, what her struggles are, or where she feels she is failing, and offer your support. People also need your support when they are succeeding. To follow up an accomplishment can at times be more difficult than overcoming the original barrier.

Support can come through a kind word, a prayer, a note, a book or tape lent, or a listening ear over a cup of coffee. I have been blessed over the years as people have come into my life to encourage and assist me. My load has been lightened by those who have taken the time to lift me up when I was down, to pray for me through a difficult season, or just remind me that they were there for me.

11
Show Them Their Strengths

You have a great opportunity to reflect reality to your group members. Take the time to notice strengths, skills, and giftedness, and tell the person what you see. Positive feedback about a strength, even one that is dormant, can release a person to invest in that area. This will, in turn, have a positive effect on the whole group.

I find that most people do not believe God wants to use them in a particular or special way. They do not believe in themselves. You can release hope in their hearts as you tell them what you see in their lives. Countless times I have taken someone aside and told him I believed he had undeveloped leadership skills or talents. I have heard someone talk about skills or strengths that she had put on the shelf because of conflicting time demands, or because someone had discouraged her. I looked for low-risk, safe places in which these people could try with little fear of failure. I am glad that many took the challenge and chose to invest themselves in those areas of their lives.

12
Defer Judgment

Wisdom dictates that we be slow to judge. In Luke 6:37, Jesus tells us not to judge one another. What a wonderful gift for others to know they can live their lives with you and not be judged. Mercy and compassion will often turn a person's heart and mind quicker than judgment and a reprimand. I have heard it said, "Dole out judgment in the same measure you wish to receive it. Dole out mercy and grace twice as much as you need it in return." Grace is a gift to us, and a gift to pass on to another. I have seen many a person whose behavior I did not approve of, or whose character was rough and crude, be greatly impacted and changed as we allowed them to grow alongside us in an atmosphere of love, acceptance, and forgiveness.

13
Offer Acceptance

Many people go through their daily lives dealing with discouragement, pressure, and rejection. By simply offering them total acceptance just for being who they are—persons loved by God— you can release grace into their lives. You can become an "island" of acceptance in their week, causing them to open their hearts to our Father who accepts us just the way we are.

Put yourself in others' shoes. Allow yourself to feel the threat, the risk, and the dread they feel. This will allow you to grow in acceptance of them, with no strings attached. If you struggle with this concept, honestly look at your own life and decide whether you deserve to be forgiven and accepted regardless of your past. This has always worked wonders in my life.

14
Show Appreciation for What They Do

People need to be reminded that there is value in their good deeds. James writes: "Faith and works, works and faith, fit together hand in glove" (MSG). Encourage others when you see them plan, administrate, assist, work, encourage, give preference to others, et cetera. We need to reward good behavior; it encourages others to put their hand to the plow. Whether you speak to them in private or in the group, you can say, "I saw what you did and I appreciate it."

15
Make Yourself Available

Let people know you can be reached for counsel, prayer, and encouragement—within bounds. By making your phone number available, or by arriving a little early and staying a little after group, you can make yourself accessible to them. People need to connect with those who are in leadership or are simply older and more seasoned in their walk with Christ. By making yourself accessible and being proactive in seeking others out, you can satisfy some of the "connecting" needs of your people.

Most people are courteous about not phoning too early, too late, or too often. If someone calls you at 11:00 p.m. and you go to bed at 10:00, you can tell them at the end of the call that you prefer not to take calls after 9:00 except in an emergency. If you are a night owl and don't mind late calls but don't want early ones, you can announce your hours of availability to the group.

16
Have Your Coach or Coordinator Call

Ask your "coach" (mentor, small group coordinator) to call a group member to encourage, challenge, or pray for them. It's important not to break confidence, but you can share nonspecific needs for extra care with a coach and ask him or her to make a call. This "buddy system" will show the person that you are thinking of him and want the best for him.

I tell the people in my group that I have a coach and that person is available to help me with issues and concerns. Occasionally when I get stumped or feel like I am in over my head, I will tell a person in my group that I am going to consult with my coach on an issue without revealing the person's name or identifying information. If necessary, I will ask permission to talk about the person's issues so I can get the help I need and or ask the coach to contact the person in question. (Remember, a confidence in a group is a treasure that you need to protect. Be careful that you do not compromise confidences as you share with your coach.)

17
Remember Anniversaries

Anniversaries are important. In this day of easy-out marriages, we ought to celebrate each one. Take the time to send a card with an encouragement. Make a big deal over the couple at a meeting close to their date. Take the time to talk about God's heart for marriage and family. Pray for the couple, and bless their relationship, inviting other members to encourage them as well.

18
Practice Unconditional Love

Almost everything in life is conditional: "If you do this, then I'll . . ." or "You can have this for only. . . ." Give the people in your small group love without conditions. Love them no matter whether they love you back or even acknowledge your love. Love them and esteem them more highly than yourself. Go to the wall for them. You have an opportunity to model our Father's unconditional love for those in the group. Know that your love is faulty, narrow, and conditional. Pray and ask our Father to give you His heart for the people in your group. Then practice loving without manipulation or expecting anything in return.

19
Mediate Differences

Your group can be a safe and healthy place to deal with differences of opinions or even broken relationships. Reading books, listening to tapes, or attending a training seminar on conflict resolution will prepare you for such an occurrence. You are not expected to fix every problem, nor is it healthy to sweep problems under the carpet. Helping others work through their differences can be a real gift. Of course, you should always know when you are in over your head. Admit it, and get help.

20
Be Dependable

It seems that there are fewer things each month that we can depend on. Government is changing, companies are downsizing, neighbors are moving away, family is becoming busier. You can be one of the few dependable things in group members' lives. You cannot take the place of Jesus, but you can surely be a signpost pointing people to Him. By being dependable, you exhibit the character of Christ and model good discipline for your group.

Do what you say you are going to do. Follow through with what you start, and be consistent. If for some reason you cannot reach where you are supposed to be, or you are not able to follow through with a commitment, be honest and communicate the change in plans. Be humble and admit you overscheduled or have a conflict. Offer to make arrangements to get the task done, or to reschedule the event. Your willingness reflects your personal integrity.

21
Lead Your People!

Leadership is a decision, a daily decision. Each day when you wake up, look in the mirror and make a decision for personal accountability, decisiveness, integrity, humility, and teachability. By doing so you are making a decision to continue to lead.

Leadership is an ongoing determination to serve God and His people. I have been in some environments where leaders were given titles, but did not lead! Leadership is practical, it impacts people's lives, it affects decision making, attitudes, and process. Leaders know they are leading if they look over their shoulders and see people following them! People want to be led by an honest, sincere, authentic, humble person who knows where he or she is going. If you have taken the role of leading, then lead.

Your leadership should flow out of a life of study and prayer. If you are struggling in your leadership, don't *do* more, *pray* more. Jesus regularly slipped away from the throngs of people to pray—to receive His marching orders for the next day from His Father. Pray hard, and choose to influence your people for His kingdom's sake.

22
First Learn, Then Teach

Teaching from the Word of God will always bring forth a harvest. The Word is a plow that breaks up hardened ground and turns over compacted soil so that the rain and sun can get at it. I believe that if you take the time to survey and explore the fields ahead of time, you will plow in greater effectiveness. Learn who your people are. Find out what is going on in their lives. The more you know and understand the people in your group (and prepare by praying for them), the more your teaching will increase in impact.

Find out how they learn. People learn in different ways and need to be addressed differently. Find out what they are interested in and what issues they are interested in studying. Occasionally take time at the end of your meeting to ask them to identify one thing they learned. Their feedback will indicate what they are taking home with them.

23
Be Patient

When I was young in the faith, I had many more questions than I had answers. I lacked wisdom and knowledge. I questioned everything: Why? What? When? Who? Why Not? I had mentors who waded through all my questions and immaturity and helped keep me focused on Christ.

Over the years, I have had many people in the groups I have led who seemed as though they should have overcome certain behaviors or sins, or should have matured more in their faith. Often, I wanted to correct, discipline, or rebuke them and tell them to grow up! More often than not, the Holy Spirit has restrained me. I have learned to be patient with people and comfortable with the work of the Holy Spirit in their lives. I know there have been times when I corrected an area in someone's life that God was not dealing with, and they could not receive the correction. There have been many other times when, after saying a simple prayer like, *God, what are you doing in this person's life?*, I have received direction or a corrective word for them that brought much fruit.

24
Encourage Apprenticeship

Invest in the people in your group. Pray hard for insight and be watchful for those who are faithful, available, teachable, and have a heart for some particular avenue of ministry. Invite them to learn how to lead, to pray, to organize worship, to study, to prepare, to follow up on prayer requests shared in the group. Give them opportunity to take part in the leadership of the group. Don't see yourself as the sole leader. If you make room in your heart and life for others to learn to lead, God will raise up others and give them similar desires. God has always had a succession of leadership, and you can play a part in training the next generation of leaders!

Jesus left us a model for raising up apprentice leaders. Take another look at His management style in the gospels and see that His model is still very culturally relevant. It looks like this:

1. *Tell them what to do.* If we take the time to explain what success looks like, most people will attain to it.

2. *Show them what to do.* You do it first. Leaders lead.

3. *Let them try.* Allow them to try it their way.

4. *Observe their performance.* Give them some room. Be watchful but don't hover.

5. *Praise progress or redirect if necessary.* Don't wait until they do it exactly right to praise them. "Exactly" is a series of partials and approximates. Praise early and for approximates. If people need remedial training, give it to them. Many of us do not get it the first time.

25
Offer Forgiveness

Two statements from the gospels have burned themselves into my mind. In the Lord's Prayer, Jesus says, "Forgive us our debts, as we also have forgiven our debtors" (Matthew 6:12). Two verses later He adds, "For if you forgive men when they sin against you, your Heavenly Father will also forgive you. But if you do not forgive men their sins, your Father will not forgive your sins." I understand that in verse 12, the phrase "as we also have forgiven our debtors" indicates a measure—or "forgive us to the extent we forgive others"! As that is the case, we need to be the most forgiving people on the planet. We need to teach, correct, rebuke, and not wink at misbehavior, but always forgive our people when they ask for it. Luke 6:38 sums it up: "For with the measure you use, it will be measured to you." I want mercy, not justice. I want to practice offering mercy and not exacting judgment. We have an opportunity to model forgiveness to our people, a model that stands in stark contrast with the world around us.

26
Help Members Connect With One Another

By purposefully helping the people in your group connect with one another, you can sow the seeds of friendship and community. When you take time to help people tell their stories by asking open-ended questions about themselves or life situations in general, you allow people to paint a self-portrait for the rest of the group. If you do this on a regular basis, the portraits take shape over time, one brush stroke after another.

I have used simple exercises to get this process going. One way is to pass out small slips of paper at the beginning of a group meeting. Ask each person to print her name, address, and phone number, fold the paper, and place it in a container. Then, sometime during the meeting, pass the container around and ask everyone to draw out a name (checking to ensure it is not their own). Ask each person to make contact with the person whose name they selected. The contact can be a phone call, a note, a greeting card, or even an invitation to meet over coffee. (Remind them of appropriate protocol if meeting with the opposite sex.)

27
Treat Them As Adults

Treat the people in your group as adults. Respect them for who they are, and for what God has done and is doing in their lives. Esteem them as peers. Guard yourself against looking at them as less learned, less mature, or less experienced. In many ways, they may be much farther along in the Christian life than you. Don't assume the role of adult or teacher, and don't think of them as children. If you do, you will either offend or belittle them, or encourage them to grow dependent on you.

Our goal is to encourage interdependence and to help people take responsibility for their own lives. Allow them to make mistakes and learn from them. Stay away from adult-to-child language like, "you should . . . you ought . . . I told you so. . . ."

Expect the best of people. Speak to them with expectation and watch them grow! Don't allow them to push you into the adult-to-child role. If someone asks you what to do in a situation in their life, don't be quick to answer. First ask, "What do you think you should do?" Let them exercise their free will, and encourage them to make good decisions. If you do offer your opinion or direction and they choose not to follow it, treat them like adults. Love them anyway!

28
Allow Failure

We need to be comfortable with failing. We have grown afraid of failure and have attached shame and guilt to failed attempts. We need to encourage failure! It indicates that someone is trying new things. If we do not strike out in faith, attempting to live our faith in new ways, we fall into a rut. Comfort leads to lethargy, which becomes stagnant life. A life without risk is like a lake without an outlet. Eventually it becomes a lagoon or swamp, and life ceases.

I have heard it said that you can spell faith this way: R-I-S-K! Allow your people to be led by the Holy Spirit and know that your group is a safe place to take appropriate risks. Remind your group that failure indicates growth and is life's way of showing us how to eliminate what does not work. If we are not failing, we are not attempting enough new ideas to accomplish a task. Let your group become a hotbed for risk-taking and celebrating new ideas.

29
Stir Them Up

Hebrews 10:24 says, "spur one another on toward love and good deeds." Left to our own devices, we will seek our comfort zone and become focused upon ourselves. Love your people enough to "spur them on" by testimony, encouragement from the Word, sharing ideas, and inviting them to do good deeds with you.

In a church I served in, we had an unwritten rule: If you do any good thing to extend the Kingdom by yourself (except when the Holy Spirit prompts you spontaneously), you are violating the Great Commission. Tough statement! But it caused us to remember purposefully to invite others to come with us and do as we do. People need to hear, but they also need to see. Jesus told His disciples what He was going to do, then He did it in front of them before He sent them out to do it by themselves.

30
Give Wise Counsel

It seems that nearly every week, someone asks me for counsel on some aspect of life. When I was younger, counsel came fast and loose, and, I fear, sometimes damaged the recipient. The longer I walk with God, the less I am compelled to offer advice or counsel. Rather, I have learned to ask this question instead: "What do you think you should do?" or "How do you feel God is guiding or instructing you in this matter?" People often already have the answer, and I then have the opportunity to confirm it and encourage them on the discernment.

When I do need to counsel, I turn to the counsel of the Scriptures, especially 1 Corinthians 2:13: "This is what we speak, not in words taught us by human wisdom but in words taught by the Spirit, expressing spiritual truths in spiritual words." God delights to guide His children, and even chooses to do so through "jars of clay" (2 Corinthians 4:7) and old cracked pots! Have integrity in your response to people's requests for counsel. Don't export what you don't live, rely on the Scriptures, and be willing to say, "I don't know" when appropriate.

31
Help Them Practice What They Are Learning

More often than not, the average person in our group (and in our church) has a basic understanding of spiritual and moral issues, but lacks a forum in which to practice it. We study and talk and debate and attend seminars, conferences, lectures, and sermons, but do not practice what we have heard. Your small group can be a laboratory for practicing the various aspects of Christ-like living.

In 1 Corinthians 14:26, Paul outlines the habit of the church when it meets together: "When you come together, everyone has [something to offer]." Paul implies that all who gather actively participate "for the strengthening of the church." Our attitude then, as we gather in the group, is that each brings something to add to the whole: a prayer, a song, a testimony, the outward sharing of a spiritual gift. It is safer to attempt to participate with others who know and love you than in the larger body of believers. Allow your group to be a proving ground, a place of reasonable trial and error, all done in order and peace. You can set the tone for the laboratory of love, and watch and guide as others put their hand to the plow!

32
Share Ownership of the Group

We all need to transition from observing to attending to belonging. The people in your group need to move in their thinking from "That's the group I attend" to "That's my group!" There are a couple of simple ways to help people make that transition. The best way I have found is to invite an individual to take on a small responsibility. It can be a short-term task or an ongoing function. Some people will "bite" more quickly than others, especially if you match natural gifting with jobs that need to be done.

Don't limit the number of jobs there can be for each person who is willing. If a person or couple always arrives earlier than the others, ask them to find their seat, get a beverage, and then greet all the others as they come. Ask them to introduce any newcomers to the rest of the group. Watch and see if someone takes lots of notes during study. You might ask that person to record each person's name, birthday, and anniversary. Then use the information to prepare greeting cards on those special occasions. Ask someone else to head the organizing of a fun night. You can ask people to accept a task for a period of time, or rotate responsibilities. Allow people to own a part of the group.

33
Be Proactive

Life not only rushes toward us at blinding speed, it demands constant reactions from us. So it is in group life. People have requests, demands, expectations, and assumptions about your leadership and your time. If you're not careful, you can slip into the rut of reacting to life and never get to the goals you have set. Choose to be proactive in your leadership. You will achieve more, you will ultimately have more energy for the people in your group, and all will be more satisfied by the whole of the small-group experience.

Being proactive takes determination, practice, and a confidence in who you are and what you are called to do as a leader. In Acts 6:1-4, we learn how the apostles continued to do what they knew they needed to do rather than allowing themselves to be distracted by the myriad needs of the people. They proactively handed authority to others who were ready, and they invested their time in "prayer and the ministry of the Word." The result is recorded a few verses later: "So the Word of God spread. The number of disciples in Jerusalem increased rapidly, and a large number of priests became obedient to the faith."

The first step in being proactive is spending time in prayer. Jesus slipped away to spend time in prayer. It was there that He was refreshed, reminded of His mission, given his marching orders for the next day. The second step is to do whatever it is you step out to do "as unto the Lord." My Irish grandfather said, "If you pray for potatoes, pick up a hoe." Pray hard, trust God, and work your plan.

34
Don't Waste Their Time

Time is our most valuable commodity these days. When people stop what they are doing, make arrangements for their children (or gather them together and bring them along), for the purpose of joining together in community, the expectation is that you will be prepared and ready to go. In Paul's letter to Titus, his good friend and pastor of the church in Crete, he admonishes, "You must teach what is in accord with sound doctrine" (Titus 2:1) and also "In everything, set them an example by doing what is good. In your teaching show integrity, seriousness, and soundness of speech that cannot be condemned" (Titus 2:7-8). These words ring clear today as the way we should live and lead. As I prepare to lead a group, three standards become my goal:

1. *Honor God.* Represent Him well, worship Him, and expect Him to change lives.

2. *Honor His Word.* It is light and life to us, so I want to handle it well and proclaim it clearly.

3. *Honor God's People.* Be prepared, pray ahead of time, be aware of what is going on in their lives, allow the Holy Spirit to interrupt my agenda, and start and end on time.

35
Provide Perspective

Perspective can be a funny thing; we lose much of our perspective at night when there is insufficient light. Without adequate contrast, the sense of proportion and depth fade, and the things around us grow or shrink. It becomes hard to navigate without stubbing a toe or falling into more serious danger.

Perspective on life is a gift you, as a leader and mentor, can offer to the people in your group. Without an objective comparison or reflection, the stuff of life can begin to loom larger than life, and important issues start falling through the cracks. By being available to reflect back to a person, objectively, accurately, and through the lens of Scripture, you provide him with a clear way of escape or a well-defined road map to get back on track.

You will want to be clear in your own mind where your boundaries are. Pointing someone in the right direction is quite different from rebuke or chastisement. Being a signpost is quite different from owning someone's difficulties and taking responsibility for their problems. Perspective is a gift—give it freely.

36
Refer Those Who Need Extra Help

Wise leaders know what they do not know! I try to impress upon our leaders that it is okay to say, "I don't know." In fact, your admission has more integrity than giving in to some demand from your ego to act as though you know when you don't. The same applies to the care we give to the people in our group and how we respond to their individual needs. It is necessary and prudent to have someone to whom members can be referred for support, care, counseling, prayer, et cetera when we have done all we know to do and don't see any significant change, growth, or healing.

One caveat to this directive is to be patient! As soon as we begin praying for someone, we invite the Holy Spirit specifically to interact with him or her. The Holy Spirit often works in ways we cannot see and do not understand. Our prayer as leaders ought to be, "Lord, I want to work and pray in agreement with you. Please sensitize me to what you are doing in this person. Help me to see the ways you are healing, correcting, or bringing understanding to him or her." Recognize that sometimes people will appear to get worse before they get better. The Lord in His wisdom knows that many of our difficulties are related to incidents from our past, to unforgiveness or other issues that attack our spiritual well-being. Don't demand that the person get well at a certain speed or rate that meets your expectations or convenience. Often they were developing a problem for years, and the healing/restoration process may take some time as well.

If you feel clearly that the person's problem is "over your head," you should get help. Be sure you don't violate confidentiality by talking about the person, except to someone in authority who is there to assist you and the person. By bringing in someone from the pastoral staff, a trained lay leader, counselor, or other trained caregiver, you offer the person a greater level of care and access to additional healing and opportunity for growth. It may be helpful for the person to remain in your group in addition to getting help from outside.

37
Evaluate the Group

A wise leader will evaluate the group every three to four months. Without evaluation based on objective information—where the group's goals, process, growth, and development are compared to biblical mandates—we fail to achieve quality goals and standards. It's a trap to assume that we are achieving just because we aren't dealing with any big problems. Quality and effectiveness don't just happen, they are the fruit of good decisions backed up with consistency, faithfulness, care, and comparison of current reality to our preferred future. We need accountability in the form of information derived from evaluation.

Evaluation is not a mystical process available only to highly skilled consultants. A well thought-out set of questions presented to group members in a relaxed manner can produce very useful results. A simple guideline is to ask questions, either verbally or in written form, which elicit honest responses from your group members. If you think anyone in the group will be offended or made uncomfortable if you ask the questions verbally, then put the questions in writing, and allow people to respond and then place the finished evaluations in a receptacle without having to identify themselves on the evaluation.

Check your progress as a group and your progress as a leader with questions like:

- ▶ Is the location and parking for our meeting place easily accessible to you?

- ▶ Does our meeting time still work for you?

- ▶ Do you enjoy being in this group? What would help you enjoy it more?

- ▶ How stimulating, challenging, and rewarding are the teaching and discussion? How could they be improved?

- ▶ What could I do to improve as a discussion leader?

- ▶ Do you feel comfortable and safe enough in our group to share about important issues in your life? What could help you feel more comfortable?

- ▶ Do you enjoy the diversity of activities (worship, prayer, outreach, service, fellowship, study, et cetera)? What would you improve in this area?

Don't let fear of criticism keep you from evaluating your group. Take the information to heart. Share it with someone in a supervisory role, and allow that person to give you objective feedback from what they see. Evaluations give you good information to digest so you can make mid-course corrections and enhance the life and vitality of your group.

38
Teach Them to Solve Problems Together

Left to themselves, groups often prefer to ignore or hide from a problem. However, ignoring a problem usually allows it to grow or repeat itself. This is often referred to as the elephant-in-the-living-room phenomenon. We can pretend the elephant isn't there and try to vacuum and carry on group discussions around it, but it becomes harder and harder to disregard the smell.

Your group will take its cue from how you respond (or don't respond) to problematic people, relationships, or situations. It is usually wise to deal with a situation head on, sooner rather than later.

Equipping Ministries International (Cincinnati, Ohio) teaches a four-step process for understanding problem situations:

1. *Identify the event or circumstance that triggers a feeling.* This event can be a situation that occurs either in the outer world or in the inner world of our mind (memory, imagination or decision).

2. *Identify the feeling(s) triggered by the event.* These resulting feelings often envelope us and seem to victimize us.

3. *Identify the behaviors with which we have responded because of those feelings.* We often think we are responding to the event, but in fact we are responding out of our feelings about the event. We call these "decisive" behaviors because they result from decisions that are often below the level of our awareness.

4. *Identify the beliefs that underly those decisions.* We have decided to respond in a certain way because of things we believe about the world and life. We have made evaluations and drawn conclusions based on our perceptions of the

event or circumstance. What are those beliefs and perceptions? Our belief system is the reservoir of our values, opinions, will, desires, attitudes, memories, self-talk, and so on.

Consider this scenario: Joe has been attending the group for several months. He has a small difference of opinion with Sue, who has been attending longer. The next week, Joe doesn't come to the group. Sue says to the group that she knows Joe is not coming back to the group because he does not like the group, especially her. The group gets in an uproar, and people say defensive things about how Joe has abandoned the group.

You can cut short this destructive process by explaining the four steps on page 35 and then leading the group through answering these questions:

1. *What was the triggering event?* Sue had an argument with Joe. Joe has not returned to the group.

2. *What did Sue and other group members feel in response to the event?* Fear, abandonment, anger.

3. *How did the group decide to behave?* Reject and blame Joe.

4. *What beliefs underlay those feelings and behaviors?* For instance, confrontation is bad and will result in abandonment and pain. Joe must be a bad person, or he wouldn't have disagreed with Sue and then not returned.

5. *What might be some more biblically sound beliefs on which to base feelings and actions?* For instance, confrontation can be constructive if handled in love.

6. *What might be some productive ways to handle this situation now?* Select someone in the group to call Joe: Sue? The leader? Pray for the group and for Joe.

39
Model Empathy

Empathy is the accurate perception of another person's feelings, and why he or she feels that way. It includes:

▶ motivation—the desire to know the person
▶ perception—paying attention to verbal and nonverbal signals
▶ feeling—the ability to resonate with the other's feelings
▶ thinking—the ability to make sense of this resonance

For instance, Barbara shares that she has to have surgery. If we are empathic, we want to know what she's feeling about this situation, and we pay attention to her tone of voice and body language to discern signals of sadness and fear. Then, instead of trying to make her uncomfortable feelings go away, we allow ourselves to feel some of the sadness and fear that an impending surgery might evoke in us. We understand that we are resonating, and we say something that validates her feelings, such as, "That sounds scary." We allow her feelings to affect us without worrying that they will overwhelm us. When people sense that we are letting their burdens affect us and that we are saying their feelings are normal, they feel connected, validated, and accepted.

An important part of empathy is taking some of Barbara's sadness and fear, and turning them over to Jesus. That way Barbara goes away with her burden lightened, but we don't go away swamped with her feelings. Empathy doesn't mean adopting someone's feelings, but simply allowing them to resonate inside us.

Showing empathy includes outward gestures like warmth in one's tone of voice, eye contact, and feedback. But while anybody can mimic those gestures, genuine empathy includes the inner state of wanting to know someone and actually resonating with their feelings. You have an opportunity to model empathy each time someone expresses fear, hurt, grief, or loss in the group. As the leader, you set the tone for the level of empathy that is expressed in your group.

One way to help your people grow in empathy is to share something in your own life that ought to elicit an emotional response, and then to ask the group what they were hearing, feeling, or thinking when you shared. Pause a moment to allow them to process, then announce that you would like to discuss the issue of empathy. Ask the group to participate in a learning experiment. Ask them to rate themselves silently on the following "warmth scale" (Key: 1-2 is poor; 3-4 is fair; 5-6 is very good):

1. Disinterested, cold, or disapproving facial expressions
2. Cool, distant, not interested
3. Mechanical or poker faced, neutral or unmoving
4. Some interest and concern shown by nonverbals
5. Attentive and interested; reflects the speakers approximate emotional state
6. Intense involvement, showing close resonance with the speaker; may touch or hold the speaker as appropriate

As group members rate themselves, explain what empathy is. Point out that being empathic is a learned behavior and a choice, but that like baseball or music, some people learn it more easily than others. Also, some people have never been encouraged to learn it. In our society, for example, girls are urged from babyhood to hone their empathic skills, while boys are often steered to focus on other skills. However, any adult can grow in empathy if he decides he wants to know people and is willing to risk letting someone else's painful feelings stir up his own. Usually, the biggest barrier to empathy is not a natural inability to feel for someone but a long habit of avoiding feelings.

Some people, of course, overempathize. Having no boundaries, they soak up other people's pain and seem to revel in carrying the burden that only Jesus should carry. Those who leap to the side of a weeping person too quickly may need to be taken aside and asked not to try to rescue people from their hurts.

You may want to have your group reassess itself periodically to see what progress is being made. Most groups I've worked with have made real gains in this area, once they understand how to cultivate such a spirit.

PART TWO:

Caring in Your Group

40
Take Time to Listen

Listening is a simple way to honor a person. In today's fast and busy world, it is hard to find someone to listen to you, even for a few moments.

When speaking with someone in your group, pay attention to your body language. Open arms and a squared-off stance are important. They say, "I'm open to you." Make eye contact. Put away distractions. Lean forward slightly. Nod your head occasionally if you understand. Ask for more definition or for information to be repeated if you miss it or don't understand.

Occasionally reflect back to the speaker what you're hearing. For example, "What I hear you saying is. . . ." or, "If I am understanding you. . . ." Checking in like this quickly uncovers misunderstandings and confirms for the speaker that his or her message is getting across.

Demonstrate for your group that there really is time to listen even to those who find it harder to formulate their thoughts aloud. You may need to stop others by saying, "Wait a moment, I'd like to hear the rest of John's thoughts."

Listening is a simple way to communicate *I care enough about you to give you some time and attention.* Your group may be one of the few places where a person can feel heard and listened to.

41
Take Time to Notice

Take the time to notice others. People feel included and encouraged when you notice (and tell them) they changed their hairstyle or are wearing a piece of clothing that enhances their appearance.

Noticing personal growth is a meaningful way to care. For example, someone who has worked on changing a behavior that was previously distracting or destructive needs to be told that you see progress being made. Look for little, incremental changes. Don't wait until the person has worked at something for months. We need to recognize and applaud small steps in the bigger process. Comments like, "I've noticed you trying to. . . ." or "I can see you've been working on. . . ." mean a lot to someone who's really trying.

One of the greatest ways to offer care to the people in your group is to simply notice what is going on in their lives. By reflecting back to them what you see God doing in their lives you encourage them to keep trying. Train the people in your group to "notice" and you will strengthen the fabric of the group as well as other relationships outside the group.

One simple way to train yourself to notice things is to talk less and watch more. When I go to a public place like a shopping mall, I like to take a few minutes to sit and watch. It is amazing to see the variety of people and to consider the possibilities of their lives. I learned this from a friend who regularly goes to the mall to pray for those he sees. I have learned to notice things that used to slip by me. Now I notice every person I come in contact with and am ready with an encouraging word. Taking notice of someone's life and offering encouragement is a simple exercise that can pay big dividends.

42
Ask About
Previous Prayer Requests

When I share a prayer request for myself or a family member, it is comforting to know others in the group are going to join me in asking God for an answer, direction, protection, or provision.

It encourages me when someone approaches me a week or two later and inquires about my request. If I have received the answer to my prayer, I get to praise God and share about the answered prayer. If I am still praying and waiting, I know I have at least one other person who is "standing in the gap" with me.

Reverse the roles and follow up on prayer requests from the members of your group. If needed, take notes to help you remember to pray and for what. It will also be a reminder later to ask about answers to the prayer. I like to jot a one-line note in my daily planner for a few days following our meeting. It helps me remember through that day to pray for that person. Prayer is one of the most powerful privileges God has given us. Use it freely, and expect results!

43
Remember Children's Names

I have a tough time remembering people's names. It is something I have struggled with all my professional life. I now write down people's names and the names of their children.

Whenever we can refer to a child by name when he or she comes up in conversation, it is a plus because people know we care enough to remember. When I encounter a group member and child at church or out in the community and can refer to the child by name, I include the child in that care as well. By simply taking an interest in a person and his family, we find new avenues for friendship and bonding.

44
Ask About Their Families

I have been truly blessed when others inquire about my daughters. By a single query, they exhibited a level of concern and interest that you don't encounter much these days. I have had others tell me that I was the only one who remembered a particular fact or circumstance in the life of their child, and that they were impressed that I would take such an interest in him or her. That connection has frequently grown into greater opportunity for growth and caring.

If you are aware of a struggle that a child is going through or if the children are succeeding in a particular area, mention that in conversation with your group member. We parents take great pride in our children and are greatly concerned about them. To know that someone else in the group is concerned about those same things and is noticing their progress or accomplishments is a blessing.

Some areas to ask about include scholastics, spiritual growth, sports, music, hobbies, and extracurricular activities. Take the time just to mention the child in conversation and watch the parents' eyes light up.

45
Ask About Their Day

We are becoming more and more isolated in our fast-paced world. We hit a garage door opener while half a block from our home, we pull the car into the garage, and down goes the door to seal off the world.

It's not a big thing to ask a person, "How was your day?" or "How's life?" "What was the high point of your day?" or "In what one way could you see God in your day today?" Before you go to your group meeting, think creatively about a couple of questions you could ask people over coffee that would send them the message that it's okay to open up. Or, before you phone a group member, ask yourself how you might begin the conversation.

Decide to change a salutation into a question. Change the question to a sincere inquiry. Then, it's important that you take the time to listen completely to the person's answer!

You may be surprised at the inquisitive looks you'll get from those you ask. It has become a norm to say, "How are you?" without expecting any response beyond "fine." Turn your salutation into, "No, really. How are you?" and watch the door to communication open between you and another person.

46
Don't Interrupt

Practice allowing others to finish before adding your comments.

One of the ways we can learn to honor one another is by discussing the importance of letting each other finish comments without interruption. Listening is a learned behavior and can take some extended time to incorporate into one's life. If a person has not learned to listen as a child, then it can take many gentle reminders and much practice to make it a new habit. Be aware and work on your own listening skills.

To find out how well you listen, ask these simple questions of a friend who will be honest with you. (You may have some ground to cover with that friend depending on how he or she answers!)

▶ When we are speaking, I am able to complete my whole thought without being interrupted.

    ❒ True most of the time.
    ❒ True about half the time.
    ❒ Actually, you seldom let me finish my thoughts.

▶ When I am sharing a thought or concern, I feel like you are fully listening and are attentive to what I am saying and feeling.

    ❒ True most of the time.
    ❒ True about half the time.
    ❒ It feels like you lose interest whenever I'm talking.

▶ When we are in a discussion, I feel that you are more focused on your next response than on what I am saying.

    ❒ Occasionally.
    ❒ Frequently.
    ❒ Amen!

Take your friend's feedback seriously, without getting defensive, and look for ways to practice actively listening to others.

Choose to stop preparing your response, even if the speaker touches on an issue you feel strongly about. Instead, fully listen to the words, and be aware of body language, facial expressions, et cetera. You will draw the person out and allow her to share her heart.

If interrupting is an ongoing problem among the members of your group, take a six-inch piece of dowel or other smooth object and write on it with a permanent marker, "The Floor." When you begin a group discussion, bring out "The Floor" and hand it to someone. Only the person holding "The Floor" may talk until he or she passes it on to another. Explain that if you think someone is holding onto "The Floor" for too long, you will wave as a sign that he or she should give it to someone else. This can be an effective way to teach people to wait and be supportive and caring listeners.

47
The Gift of a Hug

The Scriptures admonish us to greet one another with a holy kiss (Romans 16:16). In today's culture, hugging can be the application for that exhortation. Hugs convey friendship, encouragement, connecting, and love. I like to hug others; it lets them know that I'm not afraid to touch in appropriate ways. It lets other men know that it's okay to hug. Through a hug, people know we have reconnected after a period of time apart. And damaged people can learn to feel safe with me when I offer just a hug without words of advice that they feel they must respond to.

At times, a hug can take the place of hard-to-find words when we see someone in the midst of a struggle or dealing with pain. Letting people know that they can have a hug when they need one is also a source of strength and confidence-building for those who need a safe place and a warm touch.

Learning to give appropriate hugs demands we pay attention to the receiver. Some people are open to being hugged. Some are less receptive, so you may need to ask. "May I give you a hug?" This allows them to protect their boundaries and to grow to trust you. I often give a quick one-arm hug to women. Anyone who has been molested or violated in any way needs the freedom to say no thank you. I extend a warm handshake to them instead. I want them to know I am a safe person to be around.

48
Cry Together

Being committed to the point of sharing tears—crying with those who hurt—is a profound way to demonstrate care. To work at understanding them—what they are feeling and going through—to the point of tears allows someone to know that we are connected heart to heart. Tears obviously cannot be manufactured, but rather the willingness to cry grows out of a compassionate and broken heart. If you desire to grow in this area, pray a simple prayer, like "Lord, give me your heart for the lost, the broken and bruised, and those who are lonely and desperate." I have seen God answer this prayer many times, with overwhelming impact!

49
Laugh Together

I don't think we laugh enough. Church and small groups ought to be the most joyful places in town. In my group, sometimes we find it healthy, instead of an ice breaker, to share good clean jokes and to laugh together.

Laughing *with* someone, as distinct from laughing *at* someone, is a healthy way to care. A good belly laugh shared together can be a place of connecting and building friendship. I still remember certain people I have ministered to years ago because of the laughter we shared.

50
Share Your Own Needs

There is a misnomer that has become widely accepted among pastoral leaders and has trickled down to group leaders as well. This misconception is that if leaders share about personal weaknesses, struggles, or needs, this information will be used against them.

By contrast, 1 Timothy says, "Teach believers with your life: by word, by demeanor, by love, by faith, by integrity" (MSG). One of the most authentic ways to care for others is to let them see God care for you! As others see you grow, struggle, confess, forgive, and receive grace, it releases them to be transparent as well. It allows them to be real with you and with God. As I study the Apostle Paul's life, I see a man who recognized his downfalls and saw them as a reason to turn to God for grace.

Some issues, of course, are inappropriate to share. Choose wisely what you talk about, so as not to break confidences shared with you. It is not appropriate to share about personal frustrations you may have with the pastors or elders of your church. Scripture offers some strict guidelines for dealing with issues on that level. But feel free to reveal your own life in bits and pieces, and build a model for others to follow.

51
Start and Finish
the Meetings on Time

Time is our greatest currency these days, even more than money. You can honor your group members by starting and ending the group on time. Punctuality builds confidence in your leadership and encourages promptness in the group.

You can use the "soft-close" approach. Say your meeting is scheduled to run from 7:30 to 9:00 p.m., and the host is open to people socializing afterward until 10:00. At 9:00, you can announce that the group meeting is officially finished, and that those who wish may leave. Also make it clear that everyone is welcome to hang out for coffee or prayer until 10:00. At 10:00, announce that it's time to turn the house back over to the hosts. This honors the host and prevents burn-out.

52
Play "What If?"

Challenge your people's concepts and values concerning community. Refer to and use the gospels and the epistles as a basis for what Christian community may look like. Occasionally play "What if?" For example:

▶ What if we needed to depend on one another more because our economy went into a depression?

▶ What if religious freedoms as we now know them, were done away with and we were told we could not assemble freely to practice our faith any longer?

Take the time to question the level of commitment you are experiencing as a group. Ask everyone if it feels like enough.

53
Pray for Healing

We live in a fallen world and are on a pilgrimage to our eternal destination. In the midst of our pilgrimage we get bumped and bruised, neglected and rejected, invaded and infected. The small group can be a "hospital" where your people can share about their afflictions and disappointments, and receive prayer, counsel, and encouragement. If they can come to your group and know they won't be judged when they are sick or hurting, even if they brought it on themselves, you can build a portrait of God's unending compassion for them. Within the realm of your traditions, find safe ways to offer prayer with the expectation that God, through His Holy Spirit, may want to relieve the suffering, restore the person's health, rebuild the broken and bruised places, and bring glory to Himself by sovereignly intervening on the person's behalf, in the context of your group.

54
Talk About the "One Anothers"

Urge your group to show their willingness to stand together in times of hardship. You can set the example, and you may want to point out the scriptural basis for these "one anothers":

> ► Be kind and compassionate to one another (Ephesians 4:32)
> ► Serve others (1 Peter 4:10)
> ► Encourage one another (Hebrews 3:13)

Don't assume that your people understand what these mean or how they should be applying them. Take some time to discuss one of these during a group meeting. Brainstorm the various healthy and supportive ways in which you can do these "one anothers."

55
Agree to Disagree

If a relationship is built around two people always being in agreement on every issue, someone isn't telling the truth. Care for your people by agreeing to disagree on important issues and to work through disagreements in a healthy way. Don't sweep disagreements under the rug; rather, help your group learn to work through disagreements together.

As groups grow, disagreements emerge. This is normal and healthy. When I hear group leaders say, "Our group is cruising right along. We never have disagreements or difficulties," I respond, "Your group probably isn't scratching the surface, or you are hiding from real issues." I don't think a group has to be problematic, but if people are allowed to be real, there will be differences of opinion or disagreements on interpretation or application of Scripture. A group will grow into more significant community when it encounters conflict and successfully works through it.

Lay the groundwork for dealing with differences. Talk about healthy ways to deal with differences and conflict in your group. Recognize your own issues in dealing with conflict and choose to disagree agreeably!

56
Don't Embarrass Anyone

To love is to cherish, honor, and respect a person. As we teach, minister God's grace, or bring correction and discipline, we are confronted with situations where a person in our care can leave embarrassed. Protect your group members from embarrassment. There are times when the only way we can avoid embarrassment for ourselves is to embarrass someone else—to show that he, not we, made the mistake. In those situations, the generous leader will choose to protect the group member's feelings and allow himself to look bad. If the group member needs to be corrected, the leader will take him aside later for a private talk.

Even if people ask foolish questions or act out, choose to honor and respect them. Jesus' followers continually asked the wrong questions, and he was consistently patient. (Alright, He did occasionally call them "you of little faith," but He never shamed them.) Show your group members the mind of Christ and the heart of their Father.

When necessary, take time to challenge someone to think through his question or statement. An easy way to address what seems like a silly question is to answer with a question: "What do you think this means?" Encourage any response that reflects the truth and then offer additional information or instruction.

57
Ask About Work

Since we spend a large portion of our waking hours at work, it's a significant issue on our minds. Take the time to ask about a person's work: what is going on, how the person is progressing, whether she enjoys her work, how she is relating to a supervisor or those she supervises, and so on. People like to talk about themselves and their accomplishments.

You can open a door to a person's life by inquiring about some aspect of her occupation. Ask specific questions about what part she plays or how she influences her company. The million-dollar question as it pertains to work is, "What is God doing in your work life these days?" Be patient if people are not able to respond quickly. Many do not expect God to play an active role in their work lives. This question can lead to great things!

58
Don't Accept Gossip or Slander

Even the most well-meaning people sometimes slip into exchanging gossip. Sometimes it is in the form of "sharing" about another because of concern. Unfortunately, gossip or negative information shared in a group can tear it apart. Refuse to listen to gossip. Stop the person and tell him that you cannot receive the information. Ask him if he has prayed for the person over a period of time and examined his own life (Matthew 7:3). Ask also if he has judged the person (Luke 6:37) or passed this on to anyone else. If so, he may need to go back to those he spoke with and repent. If he has stood in judgment, encourage him to ask God (and perhaps also the person) for forgiveness.

Luke reminds us that we are judged with the same judgment we place on others. Stop gossip in its tracks. Do not pass on gossip about others. You have an opportunity to model holiness in this very practical way.

59
Compliment Them

Most of us go for days, weeks, or sometimes months without hearing a compliment. We hear all kinds of discouraging news reports and remarks. Often people don't recognize you as they pass or acknowledge your existence. In larger or fast-growing churches (as well as others) a person can fade into the crowd. We all need to know we add value to our church or group by just showing up.

Offering compliments to others is a skill that develops through practice and diligence. Recognize the difference between complimenting a person and puffing a person up. Look for things in his life, his appearance, or his behavior. Point those out.

Some compliments are better said one-on-one. Others are appropriate to give in the group. Proverbs 25:11 says, "A word aptly spoken is like apples of gold in settings of silver." People need to know that they are significant first to God, but also to the group. A simple reminder that you appreciate how she does a certain thing, or the way she includes others, or even how she wears her hair can make someone's day!

60
Ask Them to Pray for You

I have been led by numerous people. Most of them were people of integrity, honesty, and great leadership ability. The ones I drew closest to and trusted the most were the ones who invited me to pray for them. By revealing a need, a hope, a dream, an illness, or an area of weakness or sin in their lives, they allowed me to see them a little more clearly. By admitting they didn't have it all together, they reminded me they were human just like me. I have learned from that model and can now be more transparent with the people I lead and care for. By inviting them to pray for and minister to me, I am inviting them into the most tender and sometimes guarded areas of my life.

This model is transferable. It is said that a group cannot go farther than the leader will take it. The leader sets the pace of depth, transparency, and honesty. Opening up to be prayed for allows the others access to you in a way no other process or exercise can touch. You open yourself to the work of the Holy Spirit, and the Spirit of God is free to touch, renew, refresh, and heal in the rest of the group.

61
Brainstorm With Them

When a plan needs to be developed or a new idea for outreach, service, or fun needs to be drafted, don't do it alone. Engage the group in the process through brainstorming and let them come up with the idea. By allowing the group to brainstorm, you allow each person to have input into the making of the decision, and ownership increases dramatically.

I have used a few simple rules for brainstorming over the years. You can use these in some form to help give guidelines to your group:

▶ *Every idea is a good idea.* The only bad idea is the one not suggested.

▶ *Do not editorialize as members share ideas.* Don't say things like, "I doubt that would work around here," or "That's exactly what I think we should do!" Let each idea stand on its own.

▶ *Remember that ideas build off each other.* You can alter an idea offered by someone else by suggesting a different form or by combining ideas other people have suggested.

As the leader, you can participate in the process, but also pay attention to the rest of the group. Invite less verbal or outspoken members to participate. You may need to interrupt the process to allow the less assertive members to participate. Encourage good thinking and have fun!

62
Ask Them to Share Their Testimony

There is a special story written on the heart of each person in your group. Give your people an opportunity to share their stories. Doing this will stimulate faith in the hearts of the listeners, build confidence in the speakers' lives, and release truths they may have forgotten.

I really enjoy seeing a person sharing his personal testimony, his account of how he came to follow Christ. You can often see God do a work of renewal in a person as he is reminded of the wonderful history he has with God, and as he recounts the list of events that portray God's faithfulness.

Sharing stories of personal pilgrimage with Christ also reveals points in each person's history that give the rest of the group places to connect. As I have listened to a group member's story, I have often been amazed to discover common elements in our past or items of interest that I had not heard before. These items become jumping-off places for conversation and getting connected.

Encourage the person sharing not to glamorize his preconversion days, but also not to understate them. Also, remind the group that our testimony covers times in our lives that have been hard and wanting. To capsulize the whole of life, both victorious and heartbreaking, reveals our humanity and the thread of God's grace throughout our lives.

63
Help Them Know Why They Believe

It is important for the people in our groups to know what they believe. They need enough solid doctrine to know who they are from God's perspective, who they are outside of their relationship with God, and the ways God reaches out to them. They need to have enough of God's Word hidden in their hearts to provide them with a foundation for thoughts, words, and actions. They need the safe place of God's Word to run to when in crisis or under attack.

Equally important is for the people in our groups to know why they believe. Our propensity as Christians is to gather information about our God, our faith, our history. We can easily turn groups into learning centers rather than blending learning (which *is* valuable!) with doing and serving. Jesus said to His disciples, "If you love me, show it by doing what I told you" (John 14:15 MSG).

We need to know what we believe so we can exhibit Christ in our lives and impact the lives of those around us. We believe in order to become a different kind of people—people that love, and that reflect God's love to others.

64
Spend Time Praying Together

I am in awe of the gift of prayer. Such a simple tool, a private or public exercise that God promises to take notice of!

Prayer is a way to focus on a person's needs, problems, or hopes and ask God to intervene. The power in prayer multiplies as hearts are joined together. I believe prayer changes things. I also believe that prayer changes us as we pray. Prayer releases our hearts, and the Holy Spirit of God joins us and adds to our prayers in intercession (Romans 8:26-27) in accordance with God's will.

As we pray, the things we believe and desire are revealed among the group. Others join in agreement, and we are strengthened.

On occasion, it becomes evident that someone in the group is really struggling with the issues of the day. Or, as we worship and study together, a tender area of his life is revealed and you are presented with the opportunity to put aside your agenda for a few moments and pray for that individual. What a gift it is for that person to know he is important enough to the group to be the focus of prayer!

65
Wash Their Feet

There lies between the two extremes of leadership—boldness and brokenness—a balance point termed servanthood. This is the point Christ lived and Paul strove for. As we grow in our leadership, it should be marked by serving others. Jesus told His disciples, "the Son of Man did not come to be served, but to serve, and to give his life as a ransom for many" (Matthew 20:28). He set the goal for us: not to lord over others as leaders, but to serve them, encourage them, give them the first place, esteem them more highly than ourselves.

Wash the feet of the people in your group. You can do this literally at a special celebration, or you can find other ways to serve and bless them. Choose to honor your people by taking some time during a group meeting and telling them that you are humbled and honored to be the one who gets to serve them.

I have heard about others who look for contemporary ways to wash feet. Perhaps you can polish shoes, wash cars, or choose to do some other dirty work that gets ignored. Making a conscious decision to honor another by serving, with no strings attached, is a powerful way of showing the love of Jesus.

PART THREE:

Caring Outside Your Group

66
Meet for Coffee

In my life, coffee holds a special place. Caffeinated or decaf, steaming hot or iced, instant or steamed in an expensive espresso machine—coffee has provided me with a meeting ground for many years. Coffee seems to work for both one-on-one encounters and regular gatherings of the whole group.

In our group, coming together before the formal meeting time or staying around afterward sharing life and a cup of coffee is the norm. It is probably the simplest form of breaking bread together. When I have a warm cup in my hands, it releases something inside me, and after a week apart from my group, the connections come together again. One of the essential tasks of the person who is hosting a small group is to provide hot drinks for those who gather.

Coffee is just as effective outside the group meeting. "Let's get together for coffee" or "How about a cup of coffee?" has paved the way for new acquaintances, deepening friendships, healing hurts, reconciling differences, and subtle rebukes. By the simple invitation of sitting down in a neutral place and sharing a beverage, walls come down, prejudices become soft, and hearts open up. I don't know what it is, but the local coffee shop has greatly enhanced my relationships with the people in my group. People just seem to feel more comfortable when they have a drink in their hands. Thanks, Lord, for the coffee bean.

67
Telephone Calls

Every couple of weeks, take a few moments (I have found it usually takes only a few minutes per person) to touch base with the people in your group. And if you spread the calls out over several weeks, that's about a call a day!

Even if you don't catch people on the phone, you can leave an encouraging message. I generally call to remind them I was thinking of them, maybe touch on an issue they shared about in group, and ask if there is one thing I can pray about with them. (If you ask for prayer requests, either pray at the close of the call or write them down. Don't offer to pray unless you are willing to follow through. And remember confidentiality.)

Invite the group to get involved. Ask everyone to write down their name and phone number on a slip of paper you provide for them. Toss them all in a bowl and have each person pick one (checking to make sure they don't get their own). Instruct the group to call the person they chose sometime within the next week. Giving suggestions for the call and the ensuing conversation may help those who would otherwise convince themselves that they have nothing to say. Remind the group members that any word of encouragement is important and any prayer for blessing, wisdom, or protection can go a long way, even when prayed for a stranger!

68
Invite Them to Dinner

An invitation to be part of a subgroup of our group is often all it takes to light the fuse of someone who's either new or has been holding back. Inviting group members over to dinner doesn't need to be a special occasion. Often both the single people and married couples would just like to get together and hang out. It is a great time to discover shared history, mutual interests, and future aspirations. A simple time of prayer before or after dinner can top off the time together.

This can be a spontaneous invitation to someone from your group to go out together after church, or you can schedule ahead to have someone at your home. I find that regardless of whether we invite one person, a couple, or a number of people over, it enhances the relational cohesiveness of our group.

Sharing a meal together has had great significance throughout history and across cultures. Meals shared have been signs of agreements made, covenants drawn up, and treaties agreed upon. It can be a real honor for someone to be singled out to come to our home for dinner and conversation. The time together fuels deeper relationships, shared vision, and commitment to share responsibilities.

69
Visit Them in the Hospital

It is easy to let people fall through the cracks when they are in crisis or become sick. Traditionally, we've relied on the pastoral staff of our churches to take care of hospital visitations, but because churches increasingly draw members from large regions, and because demands on pastoral staff are also increasing, small group members become the best possible hospital visitation team.

It is important that you talk to people ahead of time to remind them that if they are going into the hospital, they need to let someone in the group know, and that information can be passed on to you. If the people in your group have not participated in hospital visitation, it is a great time to apprentice or mentor someone in the process. You don't have to have a big plan or great things to say. Simply showing up, being there, and holding the hand of the person who is ill or in for tests can make a big difference in his or her ability to cope with the situation.

As a bonus, take along a card that the whole group has signed, or even a single flower to remind the person after you have left that you were there. Visiting the sick is one of those actions that Jesus said would mark His presence in people's lives (Matthew 25:31-46).

70
Pet-Sitting

One of the struggles in leaving for a day, a weekend, or a long-term vacation is where to leave your pets. Some people are comfortable with kennels, and others have a tradition of taking their pets with them, but many find themselves in situations where neither of those options works. Offering to keep a pet is a big blessing for a pet owner, who is concerned for the pet's safety and care. If you are not able to pet-sit, then you can inquire among other group members to find out who has the room and desire to do so. Sometimes passing around a listing of people who are willing to baby-sit or pet-sit, and making that available within the group, can be a great resource for group members in need.

71
Open Your Home on a Holiday

One of the down sides of living in a transient society is that we find ourselves living hundreds if not thousands of miles away from our extended families. When my family moved a few years ago, one of the hardest experiences we faced was having to spend holidays by ourselves. When we were finally invited to another group member's home for Thanksgiving, it became the highlight of our season.

Including group members in your family festivities is a significant way to extend care to those who are lonely and disconnected from their own family and traditions. To include someone in your traditions is a wonderful way to offer care and relationship as a family. We have spent some of our most memorable holidays together with people whom we invited from our small group, workplace, or neighborhood. We find they bring different perspectives and wonderful stories from past celebrations with their families. We still recall guests who came into our lives for even a short period of time and the ways in which they enriched our celebration of an important event.

72
Invest in the Spiritual Lives of Their Children

In the religious tradition I grew up in, children were given godparents. My godparents took a special interest in my religious and spiritual upbringing and growth. They also agreed to take on that oversight in a more significant way had my parents gone to be with the Lord. In many traditions today, we don't use the word godparents, but in our small groups we can still function in much the same way.

Taking a special interest in someone's children can be a big asset to them and can deepen relationship. It's an extra special blessing when a person or a couple invests in a single parent and his or her children. Invite the children to a Christian music concert or play. Offer to help them study or to memorize a scripture. You can move into this by sharing a scripture that has become important to you. Tell the children why this passage carries extra significance for you and ask them if they have any favorite Bible sayings or stories. Pray for them, and tell them you are doing so. Ask them what they would like you to pray for them.

73
Work Together on Hobbies

Working on a hobby with someone else in your group can be a great source of fun, deepening of relationship, and gaining additional shared history. One good way to find out the hobbies of those in your group is simply to ask them to share hobbies as an ice breaker.

Inviting someone to share in your hobby can be a time of mentoring, support, and encouragement. You may find that while you know more about leading groups, the other person can teach you a lot about your hobby. A few years back I found myself working too much and not taking enough time to relax. After I shared this in a group one night, a man approached me and said he was an avid fisherman and had plenty of equipment. He offered to take me with him. I took him up on his offer and he supplied the fishing hole, pole, equipment, and bait. Because of his patience and love for me, I quickly developed a great interest in fishing and found it to be a source of fun and relaxation. I have since invited others to join me when I go fishing. Fishing has given me a source of conversation with others who are interested in this sport and allowed me a greater understanding of how fun it can be to share a hobby with someone else.

74
Attend an Event

Find out your people's outside interests or areas of social involvement—reading, theater, music, sports—and attend a presentation of their skill. Whether you announce your intention to them or just simply show up, it can be a wonderful surprise for them when they find you in the audience.

A number of years ago, a group member attended an art exhibition in which my daughter was participating. She was delighted to see this person and talked about it for a week, how this person had taken the time to come and show an interest in her craft. In most people's minds, time and interest in something that lies close to their hearts equals significant care. To attend someone's event is to celebrate him or her as a unique individual with valuable gifts.

75
Baby-Sitting

Offering to take care of a baby or a child for someone in your group says, "I see and care about your need." Both two-parent and single-parent families often need someone whom they trust to care for their child when they have an appointment or simply need a night alone. Many people find it frustrating to search for and then pay for reliable childcare. An unexpected offer to take this problem off their hands will be a welcome surprise.

If you have never been a baby-sitter, it's a good to idea to ask questions about the home you are sitting in, or, if you're entertaining the child in your home, to make sure that you have adequately "child proofed" your home so that you can protect the child—and your treasures—from unexpected mishaps.

76
House-Sitting

Offer to house-sit for a group member. Knowing you are staying in or watching their home allows them to be at ease concerning their home and belongings. Make sure you visit ahead of time so you can familiarize yourself with the layout of the home. Knowing where to find things like the electric circuit breaker box, the water shutoff valve, or the alarm system can make your time spent in their home much more relaxing as well.

77
Exercise Together

Exercising together allows you to spend time outside the group, sharing an activity that is mutually beneficial. Encourage one another, hold each other accountable, and be open to discovering a whole new side to your exercise partner that you might not see in your regular group setting. A few years ago, I committed to run with a young man I was discipling and apprenticing in ministry. It was very beneficial time: we both grew spiritually and strengthened ourselves physically all at the same time.

78
Share the "News"

As you read newspapers or magazines, allow yourself the time to cut out articles, pictures, or cartoons that might help or encourage someone in a task or strengthen them in their walk. Christian periodicals often have articles that are culturally current and easy to digest. Cut out the article, put it in a envelope, and mail or hand it to the person. I find that articles that encourage rather than correct are joyfully received. I have actually visited the homes of some of the recipients of my news clippings and found the very article or cartoon pinned to a bulletin board in their home years later.

79
Go for a Walk

Walking for fitness seems to be an enduring theme, even as many other fitness fads come and go. Add to a walk a discussion of someone's life, dreams, hopes, and frustrations, and you have a great opportunity for investment and mentoring. Spending time together this way, beyond adding to your health, can add depth to your friendship and allow you uninterrupted time to get to know one another or have an in-depth discussion.

80
Share Resources

Find a need and meet it! That's an old adage with a lot of current effectiveness. It is one way we can imitate the church described in Acts 2, when the early believers had all things in common. Sharing your time, possessions, and talents is a great way to care for others. You show them that they are more important to you than your things, and you have a wonderful opportunity to model giving and hospitality.

81
Go to the Movies Together

We are a society of viewers. We watch hundreds of hours of TV and other visual media a year. If you do a little research and pay attention to the ratings, you can pick a movie with a message. I like movies with subplots that you have to chew on to discern what is happening. For me, these are the best kind of movies to take someone to, as they are fodder for great conversations. After the movie, go out for a beverage (coffee!) or a snack and debrief. Ask open-ended questions that will allow the person to explore his or her feelings and thoughts on the movie.

If you cannot go to the movies, bring one in. Renting gives you greater flexibility because of the immense number of titles available. More than likely, a local Christian bookstore has Christian videos available for rent. Or go to your local library or video store and pick one that will be entertaining and challenge your thinking.

82
Take Them to a Doctor's Appointment

Ignorance and pain go hand in hand. I have known many people over the years who felt they were ill, or even exhibited symptoms of illness or disease, but were afraid to be examined by a physician for fear of the diagnosis. If you can accompany them to the doctor, or drive them and offer to stay, it may be all they need to vanquish their fear, and thus their ignorance.

Supporting a person in prayer is a good start, but going the extra mile to walk through a threatening situation with him helps put feet to your faith. Don't worry about knowing all the right things to say, or think you have to take away his pain. Your presence and encouragement, a handshake, a hug, and an encouraging smile may be all the fuel a person needs to propel him forward to discovery and relief or treatment.

83
Call and Ask for a Prayer Request

A good way to care for the people in your group is to call each one and ask them for one issue of concern or area of growth that you can pray about. I usually make a list of the people in my group and call 2-3 persons a week. It only takes a total of 10-15 minutes total contact time each week, and I am able to cover the group in about a month's time. When I call, I tell people the reason for the call, and if I am pressed for time, I tell them I only want a few minutes of their time. If they want to talk longer, then I determine whether I have the time or not and tell them, "Yes, this would be a good time," or "No, I am limited on time this evening, but we could set up a phone appointment for such-and-such a time."

Sometimes, when applicable, I will send an e-mail to a person in my group with my offer to pray. This allows me to initiate at my convenience and schedule, and she can respond according to her convenience.

84
Share a Good Book

We are quickly becoming a video-driven society. People are reading less because of the distractions of TV, tight schedules, and lack of discipline in their lives. I recommend books to the people in my group on a regular basis. When I am aware of a book that deals with a subject that a person is interested in or struggling with, I recommend the book to them. I also have a sizable library and have decided to make available to my group certain types of books. I went to a local printing shop and had them make a few hundred bright labels that read, "Please return to the library of Thom Corrigan." This label goes on the front cover of the book, and I find that most of them find their way back to me. I usually keep a simple list of the borrower, the title, and the date in case I need to find a missing volume later on. Many people are not aware of available books on the subjects they are dealing with, and a personal recommendation from someone they trust is a valuable tool to extend help and care.

85
Introduce Group Members to Your Friends

I love to see new relationships spring up. When there is an opportunity to do so, I like to introduce the people in my group to other friends. This allows them contact with new people, and enriching friendships can spring from these introductions.

You can also take a moment to "brag" about a specific character trait, accomplishment, or the value of your relationship with the person. Recently, I had the opportunity to make such an introduction, and I seized the opportunity to share an insight about the person in my group: "Sharon, this is Doug. We are in a small group together. I know you are interested in growing your skill as a worship leader. You ought to spend some time with Doug. He is accomplished as a musician, and when he leads us in worship in our group, we don't want to stop! Doug's heart to worship God is contagious!" In doing this, I have connected a person as a possible resource, and I have had the opportunity to point out to someone else a facet of his life that I appreciate.

86
Take a Vacation Together

Although it demands higher commitment, more planning, and prayer, an extended time together can prove to be rich. If you don't do your homework, though, it can also turn out to be frustrating. Everyone has an assumption (or set of assumptions) about their vacation time.

In my family, we wrestle with these assumptions each year. My ideal vacation plan involves some up-front planning, but little demand once we arrive at our destination. My life is busy enough with the demands of running a ministry, traveling, leading seminars, and volunteering at our church, not to mention trying to be a faithful, attentive husband and father. So vacation means lying around (the ocean, if possible) at a low-key rented house reading, fishing, and napping. My wife likes many of the same things with the addition of some shopping. But our teenage daughters look forward to lots of excitement and activity. If we add another family's needs and assumptions into this mix, the plan quickly becomes complicated.

It is possible, however, to plan a trip that two or more couples or families can agree upon, and it is well worth the effort. Make sure you discuss expectations up front, and factor them all into your plans. You'll also want to include in your plans time together and time alone. Too much of a good thing can strain relationships. Some simple, fun activities, like playing games, doing a scavenger hunt, or singing songs together can enrich your time and build long-lasting memories.

PART FOUR:

Caring As a Group

87
Build Traditions

Growing up in a family of eight in many ways was a precursor for small group life. Many of the dynamics I now practice in small groups I saw in my family—at dinner, in crisis, and at special times. We practiced some traditions passed on to us by grandparents who had brought them from other countries. Other traditions were started without a plan—by simply repeating something that we enjoyed or that went well.

I led a group and hosted it with my wife, living in a huge old home that had been divided into two spacious apartments. Our living room alone was almost five hundred square feet. As we approached the holidays and were looking for ways to reach out to others, someone suggested a feast. So we made plans to invite people in the church and those outside the church who we knew did not have family in the area. We borrowed folding banquet tables and set them end to end in our living room. We packed the room with friends, both old and new. A tradition had begun—by the end of the feast, we were sharing our thanks for God's bounty and making plans for the next "outreach feast" together.

Step out of the ordinary, out of the normal, and allow yourself and those in your group to answer the question, "What if . . . ?" or "How could we . . . ?" Simple activities can become meaningful traditions as well, if you choose to repeat them in some fashion—and then take the time to recount the blessings of previous celebrations!

88
Welcome People Back

If someone is gone for a few weeks due to a trip or illness, make a big deal over their return. An extra hug with a hearty "Welcome back, we missed you!" goes a long way. A simple hand-drawn or computer-generated "Welcome Back" sign on the wall at the group meeting can really emphasize the individual's importance to the group.

Another way to welcome people is to call their answering machine or voice-mail, and as an individual or group sing a silly song or give a big group shout of welcome. A crazy message can be a nice surprise for a road-weary traveler or a boost for someone who has been ill.

In groups I lead, I look for any reason to throw a simple party. The return of a friend is as good as any. The party does not have to become the central focus of the group meeting; it can be a simple yet significant part that leads to caring, encouragement, and fun.

89
Help Them Find a Job

One of the greatest sources of stress is facing a job change. This event can be even more stressful when we find ourselves with an unplanned job change, either because of downsizing, outsourcing, firing, or refusing to transfer. Both group leaders and members can be substantial resources to someone in this season of life by offering to forward his resume to interested parties. Other ways to assist include posting resumes in an appropriate place within your business or network, and pointing a person toward employers in his field who might be interviewing for positions.

Another simple yet powerful way to help someone find a job is simply to pray with him on an ongoing basis, asking God to provide and direct. Consistent prayer can be a huge avenue into someone's life who has not had to trust God in a large area and may be surprised to see God's provision in this way.

You may want to offer an increase in accountability in your relationship with an unemployed person. It is easy to slip into a rut of depression or become lackadaisical during a prolonged period of unemployment. By agreeing in advance, you can call the person occasionally to see how his employment search is going, or make yourself available for prayer or an encouraging word.

90
Help Them Move

Moving to a new home is a regular part of community life. The average family today moves every three to five years. Moving is often stressful and can consume large amounts of time, energy, and money. If you are willing to help someone move, and to organize the group to help a person or family move, it is a practical way to show care and support.

Organizing a group to help a member move can be a wonderful way to allow people to exercise areas of giftedness and leadership that you might not see in your weekly meetings. People who are task-oriented can rise to the situation and provide great leadership as well as managerial or organizational skills that will really enhance the move. People who are quiet but strong shine when furniture and boxes are the agenda of the day.

At the end of the move, you can celebrate someone's new home by praying for God's blessing upon the place and its inhabitants. You can even end the event by providing their first meal in the new home at the end of the day.

91
Meet a Financial Need

This one takes sensitivity and thought. When you know that someone is in need, to respond to her by helping to meet the need is a way to express love and care. This should be done through prayer and consideration, as we do not want to feed people's lack of stewardship over what they have. It is our responsibility to help carry one another's burdens, and one way we can do this is to come alongside them financially.

Sometimes we can engage the group in this process. A number of years ago, a group member was out of a job and was facing being kicked out of his apartment. We put the word around quietly to the group and were able to raise enough money to pay his rent for two months. This took a huge financial burden off the person and reminded him that, as part of our community, his need was also our need.

92
Bring Meals
When Someone Is Sick

Bringing in a meal when someone is sick in bed or one member of a couple is laid up in the hospital is a simple way we can show support and shoulder some of the burden. You can do this by yourself, but better still, you can engage the group to take care of meals for an entire week. If you have the group involved, sometimes it's good to ask someone else to organize it, allowing her to use her organizational or administrative gifts, as well as eliminating duplication of meals and effort. It is considerate to find out if there are foods that should not be brought in due to medical restrictions or allergies.

93
Sit Together in Church

Purposely going out of your way to find someone in your group and sit with them, asking them if you can share a seat or a pew with them, lets them know you count them as a friend. It allows you to share the riches of the Word being preached, to worship together, and possibly to pray together.

It might also be a good idea to invite your whole group to sit together in church, building a group identity. You can share in the worship experience together and also be on the lookout together for others to include in your small group.

94
Get Away Together

A short getaway with some or all of the people in your group can go a long way toward building deep foundations for friendship and community. I have never liked the term "retreat." Although there is, in part, a pulling back in such a time, I feel it is better termed an "advance!" I have seen great things happen when I get away from the hustle of life for even a few hours and work on building relationships, praying together, having fun, sharing meals, and serving one another.

If you do a little research in advance, you can structure your "advance" so it is easily accessible, inexpensive, and long-lasting in its impact. Don't get caught in the trap of either trying to accomplish too much or structuring your time too loosely. Do give your people opportunity for times of quiet reflection and peaceful solitude. Expect God to meet you there and for the Holy Spirit to do a great work of refreshment, renewal, reconciliation, and personal growth.

95
Throw a Party With Your Group

Instead of your regular meeting, throw a party! Ask the host/hostess ahead of time, and then invite each person to bring soft drinks, paper ware, munchies, et cetera. You don't have to make it too elaborate to have a good time. Celebrate the good things God has done or is doing. Have a few people share their stories of personal growth or triumph over a hard situation. Ask people to share praise reports concerning answered prayer. Have people share their dreams and hopes, and ask God to cover them with grace and courage to go after the dreams He has kindled in their hearts. Tell group members the good things you see God doing in their lives. Pick a few people, one at a time, and ask them to sit quietly while a few others in the group "bless" them through prayer. Have the group share with each other some positive aspect of that person's life they have noticed or experienced.

One other good idea while you're doing this is to show appreciation to the host/hostess. Let him or her know what a blessing such ongoing hospitality is to the group. Celebrate community!

96
Make Popcorn Together

Just hanging out together and enjoying simple things can bring great benefit. We can expect that where two or more are gathered in Jesus' name, He will be in our midst. So there is value in just showing up. The Holy Spirit lives in us and shows up when we do.

Spending time together increases in effect if we follow the admonition in 1 Corinthians 14:26: "When you come together, everyone has a hymn, or a word of instruction, a revelation, a tongue or an interpretation. All of these must be done for the strengthening of the church." Make this your practice even when "the church" is two or three gathered to eat popcorn and share life.

97
Serve Your
Neighborhood Together

Take some time during a group meeting to talk about service and outreach in the neighborhood where the group meets. Brainstorm together to discover the felt needs of your neighbors. Responding to felt needs may be as simple as taking their old newspapers to the recycling station, raking leaves and trash in front yards, or offering to clean out people's rain gutters. Gather as many ideas as possible, then narrow them down to a handful that you can do in one hour on a weekday evening or on a Saturday. Start with tasks that people can do with little expense, equipment, or experience. Also limit activities to those that are low risk.

The events that work best and have the highest impact are those in which you have contact with a person. Say you decide to rake the front yard of a neighbor whose yard is littered with leaves and trash. Ask everyone in the group to bring a yard rake. Bring a large plastic yard bag in which to collect the refuse. Have one or two members of the group go to the front door and ask for permission to clean the yard. You can say something like, "Hi! We're from a small group that meets down the street. We would like to rake up your front yard for you today!" The person at the door may ask "Why do you want to do that?" You can respond, "There is no charge! God's love is free, and so is this simple act of kindness. If it's okay with you, we are going to rake up your lawn, and you can tell us where to set the bag when we are done." After you finish, you may be asked other questions like, "Who are you people?" Look for opportunities, and you may be able to invite the person(s) to your group.

If you decide to take on an activity that you can do without direct contact with a person, leave a prepared slip of paper in the door or under the windshield wiper that says something like, "We did this simple act of kindness to show you God's love in a practical way. We hope we did a good job. If there is some other simple way we can serve you, please call us at this number, or come visit us on Tuesday evening for our Bible study!"

98
Go to a Concert Together

There's something marvelous about music. Music can move the heart and take the listener on a mental adventure. Going to a live performance together with a member or members of your small group can be a tremendous way to deepen community. If you are able to attend a concert with Christian musicians, all the better. There is usually a time before the concert to talk and catch up, and afterward I like to plan a stop to share a beverage and debrief.

"What surprised or convicted you during the concert?" or "What was the highlight of the concert for you?" can be the beginning of a great conversation that can lead into other areas of life.

Sharing a concert together can build a special memory for all involved. Take an interest in the music that your group members listen to. It can serve as a starting point for conversation and give you insight into how they experience life. Music makes a big impact on many of us. By being aware of it, you can enter into a discussion about what the artist was attempting to communicate and the influence it has on people. In this way, concerts are doorways to understanding and serving people more deeply.

99
Hold a Garage Sale Together

Planning and working at a garage sale with the people in your group can be an enjoyable and profitable event. By spending time planning, advertising, and executing the garage sale, you can develop teamwork, offer additional opportunities for leadership, have fun, and raise money for your chosen purpose. You may want to use the money to help pay for a group retreat, or to pay for expenses of a group member who is laid off or dealing with a long-term illness. You may want to use the funds generated by your sale to support a missionary or to help with a church-wide fundraising goal.

Many fun and productive things can happen in the planning and running of your garage sale. You will want to recruit people to head up the gathering of sale items, advertising the event, and scheduling the salespeople. Look for recruits from outside the usual core who are always involved in activities. Encourage others to be involved. Break down large tasks into bite-sized pieces so that they are easily accomplished. Just sitting together during the sale, waiting for shoppers, can provide time to talk and develop relationships. You may be surprised to see a person who has previously taken a passive role rise to the occasion and be a great organizer.

100
Cook a Meal Together

I am always amazed at what I find out about people whom I think I know when we are in situations that are out of the ordinary. I discover new and interesting facets of a person's character, background, likes, and dislikes. Cooking a meal together is an opportunity to surface people's ideas, assumptions, and habits. People have very specific and sometimes well-developed notions about how food should be prepared and served.

When you invite someone in your group to prepare a meal with you, take a little time to discuss what you are going to do and who is responsible for which tasks. You may need to go shopping together first; this expedition adds to the fun. I recently went food shopping for such a meal with a group member, and we had a blast! We had a scant shopping list but chose to improvise as we went. We ended up returning about a third of what we had tossed into the shopping basket. When we finally got around to cooking the meal, it turned into a laugh-fest. Everything seemed funny to the point of silliness, but we had a good time. I don't remember if the meal was good, but the time spent together was a definite bonus!

101
Take the Lord's Supper Together

Christians everywhere recognize the Lord's Supper (Communion, the Eucharist, the Table) as a sacrament or celebration central to the life of the gathered community of believers. In 1 Corinthians 11:24-25, Paul repeats Jesus' command to eat the bread and drink from the cup to commemorate Christ's sacrificial death for the forgiveness of our sins. Whether your tradition is to celebrate the

Lord's Supper weekly, monthly, or quarterly, you'll grow from remembering our Lord's command to keep doing this in remembrance of Him.

Some of my most memorable celebrations of the Lord's Supper have taken place in small groups. Sometimes we planned ahead and had on hand grape juice and fresh-baked bread. At other times it was a more spontaneous response after reading the Last Supper accounts recorded in one of the gospels or in 1 Corinthians. On those occasions we had to improvise. I once remember using grape Kool-Aid and Saltine crackers. Because we did this in heartfelt response to the command in the gospels, the command had the same powerful impact upon our hearts and minds, and the sharing of the "elements" was holy and refreshing for all involved.

When I have taken Communion with home groups, it was often preceded or followed by testimonies from individuals remembering specifically powerful times at the Lord's Table. Others recounted instances where the Word and the sacrament overwhelmed their souls with a sense of sorrow, repentance, and then the wash of forgiveness. How wonderful that we have this opportunity to celebrate with real elements this mystical and holy event.

In some traditions it would be acceptable for a pastor like me to celebrate Communion with my group, but not for a lay leader to do this. If that is the case in your tradition, you might consider inviting an ordained person to join your group for an evening. Alternatively, my current small group shares Communion together as we participate in the Lord's Supper in our Sunday worship celebration. This custom has helped to bond us together and remind us that God is indeed doing a holy thing among us.

Author

A former pastor with more than twenty years of small group leadership experience, Thom Corrigan is President of The Pilgrimage Training Group, the largest small group training organization in North America. Pilgrimage trains pastors and lay leaders in the essentials of strategic planning and building authentic Christian community in the local church.

Thom and his wife, Chris, live in Littleton, Colorado, with their daughters Molly and Stephanie. He enjoys listening to music, motorcycling, and fly fishing.

Turn your group into a community.

Most study guides are designed for individual use. While packed with good material, they don't provide much help in the way of group dynamic.

That's where NavPress study guides are different. By incorporating community-building questions and exercises into each session, NavPress guides will help your group grow closer relationally as you grow deeper spiritually.

Seven Traits of a Successful Leader
by Jeff Arnold

Whether you're teaching a class or leading a group, there are certain character qualities that can significantly increase your impact. This guide will help you develop the seven essential traits of a successful leader.
(ISBN: 1-57683-019-5; 7 sessions; 96 pages)

Seven Tools for Building Effective Groups
by Jeff Arnold

Just as the most talented carpenter would be handicapped without the right tools, there are key skills every effective group leader must possess. This guide features the seven most important.
(ISBN: 1-57683-020-9; 7 sessions; 96 pages)

Experiencing Community
by Thom Corrigan

Whether you're forming a new group or would like to build a stronger bond of community in your existing group, this seven-week study is the perfect "body-builder."
(ISBN: 8-09109-938-7; 7 sessions; 80 pages)

What We Believe
by Jeff Arnold

Of all the doctrines and versions of Christianity in circulation today, which ones are not negotiable? Drawn from the Apostles' Creed, *What We Believe* examines the age-old core beliefs of the faith.
(ISBN: 1-57683-071-3; 8 sessions; 80 pages)

These and other NavPress studies are available at your local Christian bookstore. Or call 1-800-366-7788 to order.

To order copies, visit your local Christian bookstore,
call NavPress at 1-800-366-7788,
or log on to www.navpress.com.

To locate a Christian bookstore near you,
call 1-800-991-7747.

NAVPRESS

BRINGING TRUTH TO LIFE
www.navpress.com